YOU ARE NOT ALONE!

TO MOTHERS OF YOUNG CHILDREN

by Chelsea J. Argyle

Written in 2003

Preface

Write a book, that has been on my checklist of "things to do" since high school. What I didn't put on my checklist, but has happened is: Become a mother of four with one more on the way. Writing a book is still on my checklist but keeps getting pushed back. Being a mother of four young children and wife of a wonderful husband keeps me busy. I thought life was busy working full time and going to school full time—wrong. You don't know what busy is until you realize you can't even go to the bathroom alone.

I always thought I'd write a great romance/suspense story. You know, the ones you can't set down and when you are able to get away from them you daydream of what's going on in the story. Well, my dreams have changed. Don't get me wrong, I still enjoy well written fiction, but I also enjoy being a mother.

What credentials do I have to write a book to inspire mothers of young children? None, except that I am a mother of young children. That's why this book can't wait any longer. Pretty soon I won't be. These children just seem to keep growing and at a very fast pace too. My goal in writing this book is to let mothers know they are not alone, even if the only mother who reads it is my daughter or one of my sisters. This last year my sisters both had their first child. I think of them often and feel a rush to finish this book for their sake.

Chapter 1

In The Beginning

Life looked promising, I had just graduated from high school, I was leaving in the fall for college and I had my life planned out. That was my first mistake—planning. Lesson number one: Make plans and then expect them to change. I met my husband before I even left for college. Of course neither of us were "ready" for marriage yet so it didn't matter that we fell madly in love with each other—right? Wrong! I did go to school one year. We were married the following summer. We then "planned" to get schooling behind us before we had children. There we go planning again. On our first anniversary I was seven months pregnant.

My first visit to the doctor with the pregnancy required filling out forms. I started to put down my age—19. I stopped, looked at my husband and told him we had to leave. He looked at me a little puzzled. I then informed him this was a teen pregnancy and we had to come back in a couple months, after I turned 20.

Despite being 19, I began to receive motherly instincts in me and got excited to have a little baby. Of course, along with feelings of joy came anxiety. I was going to be responsible for another human being for a very long time. What was I doing? Would I be a good mother?

I was working full time at a real estate office and going to school full time. I couldn't imagine being at home full time with a child—what would I do all day? I enjoyed working and school and told my boss I would keep working after the baby was born. The months flew by despite swollen feet and growing pains. The beginning of November I had a beautiful baby girl. After one week of being home with her, I couldn't imagine leaving. I cried at the possibility of going back to work. How could a child who kept us up at nights totally exhausted make me want to be with her so much? I was in awe as a mother. I would rock her in my rocking chair each day, once I was able to sit normally again, and tears of love and appreciation for her would come. Oh, how I enjoyed that time alone with my little baby. My miracle! I appreciate that time more now because I know how short lived it is.

Oh the pains we go through in this life. I am learning to be thankful for my trials—they all bring good things into my life. Think of carrying a child for nine months and then the delivery process. (Thank goodness for modern technology, otherwise I think I would have died in that process—pain and me just don't mix.) Face it, bringing a baby into this world is a trial—but then the child is set in your arms and your heart will never be the same again. The joy far outweighs what pains we went through—it must or I wouldn't have done it three more times and be doing it again right now. My doctor once told me that women have amnesia or they would only have one child each. Maybe that is true, but there is a joy in motherhood that far outweighs the pains. I love being a mother!

I must admit I haven't always felt the appreciation I feel now of having the opportunity given to me to be a mother. Having three children in 2 years and 9 months took its toll. I was pregnant with my third, attempting to potty train my first, trying to get my second to walk and not seeing much of my husband since he worked full time and was attending school. This was a time when I literally cried everyday, most of the day sometimes. I remember my three-year-old daughter saying to me of this time, "Mom, remember when you cried every day?" I look back now at that time and wonder what I could have done to better enjoy that period in my life—thus I hope I can give others insight to how they can enjoy their young children.

I remember being so lonely, no one to talk to, if only I had realized there are so many others going through the same struggles. We have a worldwide support system of mothers, why can't we get together, learn from and strengthen one another.

My first three years of married life was an experience, not that life doesn't continue to be an experience, but as my husband would say, "—let me explain." First of all you need to understand I am a very religious person. I have a close relationship with my Heavenly Father. Each decision my husband and I make is made prayerfully. The decision to have each one of our children was made that way. After I had my first I did continue to work. I had a wonderful boss who offered to let me bring her with me. About the time my baby was nine months old I felt I wasn't giving enough attention to my work or to my daughter. After much prayer and pondering my husband and I decided to have me quit working. The only problem with this was that we weren't sure how the rent would be paid with out my income and little did we know that number two child was already on his way. One night, after I had quit, we were on our knees desperately seeking some answers as to what to do and the phone rang. It was a friend letting us know about an opportunity to live in a mortuary. "A mortuary?" you say. Yes, a mortuary. The rent was free and we were paid for some of the services we performed there. It was a good experience for us.

We had our second son while living in the mortuary. Just before he was born, my husband got laid off from his job. The mortuary became an even greater blessing at that time.

A year later I was expecting my third, Rex had received a job, but it was further away. We then had the opportunity to move into his Grandma's house while trying to sell it for the family. It was closer to where he was working. This was a good thing for us, but the house itself added a bit more stress since there were other living things trying to share the home with us; like mice, snakes, a squirrel and birds. Before we moved in Rex had fumigated the home. Rex's grandma, bless her heart, had been living there by herself. It was an old home. In fact both of Rex's parents had lived in it at some point during their childhood. There were fields all around so mice came in and out where they could. It was located near a lake thus the water level was high and it became a perfect place for snakes, especially in the crawl space beneath the house. There were huge beautiful trees all around, the only problem with this was that mosquitoes liked the cool shade of the trees also. I hate to put this house down because it had been made a nice home for Rex's grandparents and it had a lot of memories especially for Rex's mom and her siblings. It was just an old home that had been neglected for a while. The snake problem probably could have been controlled. It's just that when a snake came in the house, Rex's grandma would throw it out instead of getting rid of it, thus they began to multiply.

When we first moved in we didn't have many problems since Rex had fumigated. One day we were having a family come look at the house who were interested in buying it. I had gone into the bathroom behind the kitchen, when I came back out there was a snake in the middle of the kitchen floor. I screamed and jumped up on the counter. Thank goodness Rex hadn't left for work yet. About the time I screamed Rex noticed the people pulling up who were coming to look at the house. Rex got a shovel and took care of the snake while I answered the door. I believe it was this couple who actually ended up buying the home. This was the only time a snake came up into the house but we saw them constantly out in the yard.

Another evening Rex and I had put the kids to bed and were playing a game together at the kitchen table. Out of the corner of my eye I saw something move by the fridge. It was bigger than a mouse. I told Rex a squirrel had just run into the bathroom. He didn't believe me. He searched for it, but found nothing. We kept on playing and it eventually came back in. I got Rex's attention and he was shocked to say the least. His reaction was actually quite comical as he tried to chase it. We never did catch that squirrel. At least we found humor in trying.

We started building a home. This was another stress in itself, but I was excited about this one. We had found a quiet neighborhood much like the one I had grown up in with an elementary school just down the street. Luckily my husband has good taste, probably better than my own because by this time I was in no condition to think clearly and make good decisions. Rex pretty much picked out what our house would look like and he also spent many hours working on it. By this time I had moved in with my mom and then later stayed at his parents house a couple hours from where we were building. We saw Rex on the weekends.

The reason I mention these events throughout these three years is to bring attention to the fact that we don't just have the stress of being a mother, but of life. By the time I had my third, was living among mice and snakes, trying to make decisions in building a home and having to make it all match up financially. My last straw was about to break. After we moved into our new home I was fortunate enough to meet some other mothers who I became close friends with. This is when I discovered I wasn't alone. There were other mothers who were lonely. Not only did I discover others were lonely but also going as crazy as I was. Together we helped each other. Hopefully at least one of us was having a good day at any given moment. I feel that I became a better mother as I watched my friends and then discussed concerns with them. This was a support group, a group of women who could express joys, triumphs, and frustrations of being mothers and totally understand one another.

When I initially moved into the neighborhood I was in a desperate state. I had gone from living where there were few people around me, especially my age, to a subdivision full of young families. I was anxious to make friends. I got a phone list of families who attended my church in the area and began calling mothers. School was not in session at the time so we arranged to meet at the school playground each Friday, enjoy sack lunches and let our kids play. The best part of it was that we were able to get to know one another and talk as mothers. Friendships were made and loads were lightened as we discovered we were not alone.

Wherever you are or whatever your situation, find a support group. Church is a good place to start. That is where I got my initial list of mothers to call. If you are in a neighborhood or an apartment with lots of young mothers, go door to door. If you are out in the middle of nowhere go to town. Try the nearest library. During story time you will usually find a few other mothers. Wherever you are, look for others with young children, take a deep breath and dare to approach. Invite others to your home or a certain park weekly. In my situation, my husband usually had our only vehicle so I had to find somewhere I could walk to. Don't wait until you are desperate, find your support group early. It would be nice to have this support group in place when you are pregnant with your first. Why not find a group of mothers before yours is born, just remember to not judge until you have as many children as the one you are watching. I would imagine if you are reading this book you are already past this point, but it wouldn't hurt to mention it to other pre-moms. I am not saying having friends in similar situations takes the trial of motherhood away but it does help make life bearable and even quite enjoyable at times.

I mentioned to not judge until you have as many children as the person you are watching. After I had my second I would be up and ready for the day before my kids woke. Make-up, hair, I was ready to meet the day. One morning about 10:00 we were out on our walk and I stopped by my neighbors to drop something off. I was astounded to find her children still in their pajamas and the mother still in bed. "What kind of a mother was this?" I thought.

It was a mother with three small children. Who knows what her specific challenges were, I never got to know her well. I am now expecting my fifth and quite often find myself in my pajamas at noon. Some days my greatest desire is to just be able to shower sometime during that day. I often think of the judgment I so rashly made on a dear mother who probably could have used my help that morning instead of my harsh judgment.

So, let's work together as mothers. Reach out to a mother in a grocery store with a child throwing a fit. Let her know you understand. Don't just walk away thinking, "Boy, I'm glad that's not my kid." Because most likely next time it will be. Sometimes I have to chuckle when I see another mother's child act up—it makes me feel like I am not the only one. Be the one to go to that mother and let her know she's.

Chapter 2

STAGES OF MOTHERHOOD

The way I see it there are stages in being a mother starting when you are born. When my first son was born my daughter was 17 months old. I couldn't believe the motherly instincts in her. I wrote in my journal at the time:

Alexis loves Jordan and is really good with him. He is always the first person she wants to see when she has been away from him at Grandma's or if she has been asleep. She gives him kisses all the time and is amazingly kind to him. Sometimes she pokes a little too hard or won't leave him alone when he is trying to sleep, then we have to get after her to leave him alone. She has not been mean to him at all that I have noticed. When she first saw him at the hospital and we told her it was her baby to take home she just giggled and jumped up and down. She was so excited to have a baby. When he cried, she looked like she was going to cry too. What precious children we have.

My daughter has always been motherly with her brothers, sometimes a bit too much. I have to remind her every so often that I am still the mom.

It is during this stage a child will play with dolls, stuffed animals, whatever can be found to take care of.

Often at this time, as a parent, you see and hear your child mimic you. This can be good or bad. Watching your child carefully rock a baby and sing sweet lullabies of her own making is good. Seeing her point a finger and chew out a baby doll can make you cringe.

Riding in the car one day my daughter began yelling, "Lady! Lady! Watch out Lady!" Confused at what she was doing, I asked her to stop. A couple of days later we were in the car as a family and my husband got upset at a nearby driver. I then realized what my daughter had been doing and why. This made me laugh. I related the experience with my husband. I have since shared this story many times much to my husband's dismay.

One thing I like to do is write Thank you cards. I did this as a New Years resolution a couple years ago. I decided to write at least one Thank you card a week. This helped me have more gratitude for others in my life and I have since continued except not quite on a weekly basis. My Daughter just turned nine-years-old. She was blessed on her birthday with gifts from extended family members. I was a proud parent when I came home one day and my daughter had made cards for those who had sent her gifts.

Okay, for the sake of my husband I better put in a good note for him. Boys also will imitate their fathers. My two older boys enjoy their dad a lot. The younger of the two I have seen often try to imitate the way his dad is sitting or resting his arms when watching television. The older one has taken on his dad's love for reading and gaining more knowledge. We often have to pull his head out of a book to get him to finish jobs or be wherever he is supposed to be. I was amused the day I saw one of his books on the bathroom counter, one of the places his dad reads.

As I got older the next stage set in and that was babysitting. Being the oldest of four children I babysat more than I liked, but I did enjoy watching other people's children.

I watched other mothers and made a picture in the back of my mind of what kind of mother I would be and of what motherhood would be like. I remember helping with laundry and while doing so pretending I was the mother. It was much more glamorous then. There was a family with two children that I would stay with for whole weekends at a time. I would keep the house, vacuum, fix meals, get them ready for bed etc. I even was left a car after I turned 16. This, to me, was the best! I also remember standing in front of the mirror wondering what I would look like pregnant.

Of course, I didn't think motherhood would come for at least ten years from that time. I had big plans in my head to finish college, including graduate school, before I married and had children. I know I didn't picture the laundry I was doing being bedding from a sick child and I know I couldn't feel the growing pains as I wondered what I'd look like pregnant. On the other hand, I could never have imagined the feelings of love I would soon have for children of my own. That is something that can never be explained, only experienced.

As a new mother I was entering the next stage. This is the stage of being a "perfect" mother. I had many expectations and certain do's and don'ts I was sure to live by. Such as I wouldn't use a pacifier (binky, plug, etc.). That one lasted until my daughter was three days old. The pacifier didn't leave her for over two years after that. Another was I wouldn't use the word "No!" Instead she learned quickly how to say "Do!" with a long O sound for don't. I also decided I would not spank or hit our children. That one I still try to do, but there are moments when my hand has been quicker than my brain.

This stage was hard because I had a perfect picture in my head of what kind of mother I was going to be, but being woken at two in the morning by a screaming child didn't fit in that picture. I think to be a "perfect" mother you must have sleep, which rarely happens on a regular basis with a newborn. I remember thinking I would never have another good night's sleep again in my life—it was exhausting! (I have since had some good nights of sound sleep.)

The shorter this stage, the better. Once you realize you won't be perfect and it's okay, you can become a better mom just by not putting yourself down with such thoughts. This is where my religious beliefs take over. I truly believe if I do my very best there will be help from above to make up the difference.

I recently read a quote by David Frum, a Jewish speech writer for the Bush administration, regarding President George W. Bush and the confidence he leads with. The book quoted Bush from a speech he gave in May 2001 at the commencement address for Yale University. Bush was a former student of Yale. "When I left here, I didn't have much in the way of a life plan. I knew some people who thought they did. But it turned out that we were all in for ups and downs, most of them unexpected. Life takes its own turns, makes its own demands, writes its own story. And along the way, we start to realize we are not the author." "And that," the author states, "was why Bush was so confident: not because he was arrogant, but because he believed that the future was held in stronger hands than his own." (David Frum, "The Right Man," New York, Random House, 2003, pg. 30)

It is this realization that can make us be the best moms we can be. Knowing the future is held in stronger hands than our own, all-knowing hands. We have our free agency to lead our lives in the direction we choose, but realizing who we are as daughters of God and knowing the children we have are not only ours but children of this same God, brings an assurance that is needed in motherhood.

During the stage where my first three children were under the age of three I can't say I was enjoying motherhood. It had its ups and downs and the downs outnumbered the ups, but the ups are worth suffering through the downs. It is this stage where a support system is needed the most. I was lonely at this time in my life. I yearned for a friend, someone to talk to. Someone to say, "It's okay, you're not alone in this." Someone to take the stress of my behavior off of my husband. It was this stage where I felt I had no one to talk to. I was married young and most of my friends I'd grown up with were still single. My sisters were young and living their own lives and my mom worked and still had kids at home she was raising. This stage is the reason for writing this book.

There are other stages as life goes on. I am in another one of those right now as I have three children in grade school. Life keeps getting busier, but I hope as life goes on I am learning to treasure the moment, for I will never have another "stage" like it with my children.

And by the way, I am loving this stage despite trying to keep up with four kids and a pregnant body. Your goal: to enjoy the stage you're in for it is just that—a stage and it too will pass.

(Note: I do have bad days, but remember I have a group of friends to rely on. My worst days are when I keep to myself and don't turn to these friends.)

Chapter 3

BE A FRIEND

As a young mother and being so lonely I remember wishing someone would come by, knock on the door, be my friend and make my life better. What I now realize is that I was actually surrounded by people who could have been my friends, who I could have opened up to. I closed myself off from others. I didn't want others to know I wasn't "perfect".I kept a clean house, my children were dressed to look good, clean faces, matching outfits, hair combed. A great appearance was made, but inside I was hurting, longing for someone to open up to. There is a song Michael McClean wrote that I remember listening to at the time and understanding how the girl in the song felt, "Which Part Is Mine?" It's a story of a girl growing up trying to understand what part in life was hers.

Everybody said she could work wonders,

And she wondered what everyone meant.

She played so many roles—it was taking its toll—

And she feared that her time was misspent.

The girl opens up to her husband and then at the end of the song opens up to her Heavenly Father who in turn gives her the answer she is looking for and she ends the song saying:

After I've done my best

I know you'll do the rest.

(Michael McClean, CD The Collection Vol.1, Salt Lake City, Utah, Deseret Book, 1994)

This goes back to trusting in a Heavenly being which it helps to have a friendship with. We also should allow ourselves to open up to others. I have since learned that by putting my trust on the line and allowing others to see my weaknesses, I actually receive strength through their friendship and then they, in return, trust me to their weaknesses. This allows me to know what I can do to help them and be a better friend.

Trusting others and allowing them to see our weaknesses is not always easy to do especially if you have been hurt and betrayed by someone you opened up to. Actually, this is not the easiest thing for me to do. Opening yourself to being hurt again is hard but remember you are also opening yourself up to being loved. I can't promise you won't get hurt again, but the chance is worth it when you do finally meet a friend you can trust. I have met others who have a hard time trusting—they want so much to be your friend and serve you, but are very cautious about letting you know of their personal circumstances. It's hard to have a close relationship when the communication only goes one way.

It's also hard to be close friends with someone who is mainly concerned about what you can do for them. You feel used. Remember a good friendship goes both ways. Not everyone is going to become your closest friend, but hang in there, everyone needs a friend and along the way you'll come across a few that you will wonder how you ever got along without.

Remember also that we all make mistakes. There are times we may be upset with a friend, but don't let that ruin what friendship you have. Talk it out, forgive and forget where necessary.

Not long ago I was informed I was on someone's list of "perfect people". My wise friend who this was admitted to was kind enough to let it be known that I was not perfect. Wasn't that nice of her! We began to embrace this person with the "perfect people list" and allowed her to discover for herself our "imperfections". She is now a dear friend of mine who has helped me when in a bind more than once.

This is a motto of mine—If you think she's perfect, you don't know her. Get to know her, don't hate her for what you don't know. If you think she's perfect she must have qualities you admire, get to know her and learn how you can acquire the same type of qualities. Remember each of us are unique and have different talents and strengths. Don't forget to realize you have strengths she may not have. This is what is so wonderful about relationships. Whether it be a spouse or a girlfriend you can thrive on one another's strengths.

My husband and I just took a short personality test. Four questions were asked. We were opposite on all but one. We get along great and have been told our personalities complement one another. One of my closest girlfriends and I were answering questions regarding the roles we play in life. We have a lot in common, yet on some questions we were totally different. I enjoyed answering these questions with her because we would read a role like: The Loner, "Always proving he doesn't need others. Has learned to become self-sufficient. Very sensitive and caring. Detaches his feelings. Feels guilty for wanting love and denies his needs. Needs are signs of weakness." We read this and fell silent for a few moments. I knew this was a role I played frequently. Finally she says, "I'm sorry, but you do this." Do you know how good it felt to be able to answer these honestly not only with myself but with a friend. We are able to help one another by the different views we take.

We don't try to hide our weaknesses. We encourage one another to do better and become more.

My life has truly been blessed with good friends. Opening my heart and allowing others in has brought an abundance of blessings. As I see a need I try to serve my friends the best I can. The service has been returned to me ten-fold. The scripture James 5:16 says, "Confess your faults one to another, and pray one for another, that ye may be healed. The effectual fervent prayer of a righteous man availeth much." Confessing my weakness to my friends and allowing them to help me has blessed my life and they have been answers to my own prayers. Shortly after I had my fourth I was having back problems and couldn't clean my house like I wanted. I then became quite ill with an infection. I was tired, frustrated, and just plain discouraged. A couple of my friends noticed and came over to clean the house. This brought such feelings of love and I truly appreciated their sacrifice for me.

Another time my house was cleaned by friends was a time when I actually asked them to help. I had recently found out I was pregnant and my husband and I decided to put our house up for sale. I was sick and exhausted and now had to have a house ready to show buyers. I held a cleaning party for myself. We enjoyed a morning of cleaning together. It wasn't easy for me to ask others of this, but what feelings of love came from those who responded in such a positive and caring way. It is definitely worth your time and effort to try to make friends. I enjoy when a friend calls a girls night out. This is the best time to see a "chick-flick" and share laughter together or designate a place to meet for dinner. This type of activity helps me get to know others better. I have also been invited to weekend retreats which are fun and allow for a lot of open conversation.

I personally enjoy inviting a few mothers over for lunch just to get to know them better. I think of three or four ladies to have over and call each one (sometimes I have to call 10 just to get a few who are available). I usually plan this the morning of so it is short notice and little planning. It's not fancy—those who know me know I am not much of a cook. My husband does the cooking for company in our house. Usually those I call offer to bring something, sometimes I have a meal all planned out and they don't need to bring anything, but other times we can throw a nice lunch together without any painful planning. I like to have my house straightened, but I don't do extensive cleaning—that would make it not worth doing! Let them see you for who you are. Better yet, allow them to feel better about how their house may look.

My husband and I enjoy having another family over for Sunday dinner. This too is a way I have come to know others. My husband does most of the planning for this so it is not a stressful thing in my life.

Don't put yourself down by others who seem to have it all together. Get to know them and most likely your life will be blessed by gaining another friend. In visiting with a neighbor she expressed to me how she is haunted by a lady who she feels is perfect. Her house is spotless, the kids are perfect, each hair is always in place. As I listened to her all I could think was you don't know her—not all of her. And maybe this lady won't let you come to know the true her, but you can keep trying by just being a friend. We shouldn't judge. With my experience when something looks too perfect there is more to discover. One thing I have discovered in trying to get to know others better is that everyone, without exception, has problems. Some problems may not be as visual as others. Health is usually a problem hard to hide. Some problems may be inside—anxiety, depression. On the outside all looks well and fine, but inside there is such pain and hurt. Maybe there is a problem in their family. Worry over a child, a parent, a spouse. Maybe there is a physical pain they are attempting to hide. I know I get pretty ornery when I don't feel well. Quite often there are financial worries in life. I haven't had the problem of having "too much" money, but I have seen the stress of wealth in others' lives. The list goes on and on. We each have our different worries and strife. Not all problems are the same, but they do exist in the lives of all of us. We could all use an extra friend, be one and you will be blessing both of your lives.

Compared to a time when I had no close friends to confide in, especially as a mother, I feel truly blessed by the friends I have gained in my life in the last few years. Be a friend, blessings will flow back as sweet friendships are made!

Chapter 4

TREASURE THE MOMENT

Reading my journal I came across a paragraph which mentioned the awful duty of cleaning out the tub when my baby had messed in it and then in the next sentence, same paragraph, commenting on how precious my child was. These two sentences did not go together. This is part of the miracle of being a mother. You cherish your children despite the "messes" you are called on to clean up.

Ideally I like to rise early and be ready to face a day with a face others don't mind meeting, but sometimes situations don't allow it. Like a night with no sleep, waking up to a sick child, a phone that won't stop ringing, a child that won't stop crying or worse waking up with yourself not feeling well and still having to deal with all of the above.

Every so often I am able to make a day great by rising early and getting a lot done, but usually my best days are when I have allowed myself to go with the flow and enjoy a moment with my kids. Allowing myself to stay in pajamas because a child asked me to play a game or read a book to them.

Take time to make moments happen. In the winter we have been known to have picnic lunches. We spread a blanket on the floor in the kitchen and enjoyed our picnic with the snow falling outside. Another fun activity is to get your popcorn popper, take the lid off, put it on the blanket and allow the popcorn to fly. By the way, a popcorn popper is not the microwave—I got my popper for my wedding, I don't know if people still buy these. We enjoy ours.

Quite often, especially when I have a house full of neighbor kids I will make up a batch of playdough. I like homemade playdough much better than store bought—it seems to be much cleaner, not as crumbly. Kids will spend hours using their imaginations especially when you sit down with them and they have someone to share their inventions with.

FAVORITE PLAY DOUGH

2 ½ C.	Flour
½ C.	Salt
3 TBSP.	Oil (baby oil works best)
1 TBSP.	Alum
2 C.	Boiling Water

Put dry ingredients into large bowl and mix. Combine oil, boiling water and food coloring. Stir dry and wet ingredients together until mixed well. Keep in a covered dish or sealed bag.

Go on a nature walk. I love to go walking. Put your kids in a stroller or if they're old enough let them ride their bikes while you walk. With my first three children I had a single stroller that I literally wore out. I would sit all three in it. It was the kind you could lay back and allow a child to lay down. I would sit each of them in it with their legs around each other. We would walk all over. After a rain storm we would see worms or in the spring look for new flowers sprouting. The kids love to see animals, especially when a baby horse is in the field.

When our trampoline was up and working I would put on my swimsuit, much to my neighbors dismay, and jump with the kids while the water ran on us. I am surprised this didn't cause any privacy fences to go up.

In the winter go out and play with your kids. Pull them in a sled or have them try to pull you. Make a snow fort. Play a snow game—follow the leader through new tracks made in the snow. Make it a family activity and include Dad on a day he is home. We have made many snowmen or snow angels. My kids were so excited for the first snowfall this year because we had read a book about a little girl's memories of playing in the snow with her grandfather. From the book we learned how to make snow chickens and snow sandwiches. Snow chickens are made like snow angels except you don't move your legs, just your arms. You then put a glove above the head for the comb of the chicken and a carrot for the beak. Snow sandwiches are made by sprinkling sugar on two slices of bread, holding them under the falling snow, putting them together and eating quickly.

It is also fun to invite a friend and her kids to do any of these activities with you. My kids get so excited when they find out friends are going to join us.

"Out of the mouth of babes." I love to hear what children have to say. My son was a vampire for Halloween. His dad had done his hair in what he calls a "but-cut" where the hair is parted in the center and pulled away on each side. My son proceeded to tell me and my mom that he had a "but-crack" hair-do.

In our house we have "panicakes" instead of pancakes. It's fun when a child is learning to talk and gets words a little mixed up. I love to hear a young child say new words. Brancra for Grandpa, Dancu for Thank you, Thingers for fingers and Free for three. What precious moments!

My husband and I had recently had a family meeting on what type of words we use in our home and vocabulary. I got a phone call from a neighbor that her son had come in upset because my son couldn't play with him any more because he was using bad words—the "D" and "S" words. I asked what the "D" and "S" words were—dumb and stupid. I proceeded to explain and told her I would take care of it. While I was on the phone my son had come to tell me he had to talk to me in private. We discussed the situation. He was devastated and told me the neighbor friend had promised he would try not to say the words anymore. He was soon reunited with his friend.

My husband tells me he's not going to have any words left to say soon because I am always saying such and such a word doesn't sound good. When he was mad at the cat and called her dumb the kids got after him. He said, "Well she can't talk can she." We had recently explained the meaning of the word dumb from the scriptures so the kids understood.

Another story along these lines was with another neighbor friend. He was playing Nintendo with the kids and I think the word he was using was "Suck". I commented again on how it just doesn't sound very good and lets not use it in our house. A little later I looked outside and there were huge hailstones falling. I called all the kids upstairs to see the hail. My neighbor kid then tells me, "Well my mom doesn't let us use THAT word." I tried to explain the difference between hail and hell, but eventually gave up and said, "Look at the big snow then!"

Make traditions in your life that the kids will treasure. I was surprised as we discussed what we were doing for Thanksgiving with our children. My son was disappointed we were going to one grandma's instead of the others. I told him we would see the other grandma that evening. He was still disappointed. When I asked him why he said, "Because I wanted the nut cups." This is a tradition in my husband's family. Every year creative nut cups are made to be filled with mints and nuts at each place at the table. So we decided to carry this tradition on and make them ourselves for the other side of the family.

Allow your children to let you know what kind of traditions they want to start. As we were coming into the holiday season we sat down with our children and asked them what type of things they wanted to do for the season. The things mentioned were activities we have done in the past that they want to do again. This is how traditions start. Something as simple as reading a Christmas story each night was remembered.

All year long the kids look forward to camping with their cousins at a reunion we have each summer. We pitch our tent right in their grandparent's yard. Of course it helps that their yard is about 20 acres and includes fish ponds. We also have the tradition of going to the town my husband grew up in for the 4th of July. We enjoy the small town parade that is fairly short and has lots of candy thrown out. We have annual trips we take with my parents such as a week at Bear Lake. We usually do this the week of my son's birthday so he calls the cabin where we stay "His" cabin. These traditions are things our kids talk about constantly. They are things we treasure.

Our children often feel our stress and know we too need extra love at times. On one stressful day my daughter, then only a year and a half, put her arms around my neck and proceeded to hold me for a while. She knew what I needed.

Being pregnant with my fourth, my daughter saw me picking things up and scolded me. "Look at you bending over, let me do that." She proceeded to help pick up toys.

Our children need to feel extra love too sometimes. Each morning I am woken up by at least one of my kids crawling into bed next to me. They love to come and snuggle for a few minutes before we start the day. Occasionally when a child will sleep in and we are already up they will complain because they didn't get to lay in my bed with me. When my mom had the opportunity to come stay overnight with my kids she commented on how she wished she could've had a picture of all four of my children lying in bed with her. It was a moment for her to remember.

Take these moments and cherish them. Write them down and have them available to read on a day when you are not cherishing your child so much. I have on my computer a journal for each of my kids. When they accomplish something or say something which makes me laugh or even cry I try to write it down. I especially enjoy writing about frustrating moments because it is later I can laugh over what happened. When my children have kids of their own I will give these journals to them and allow them to have some laughs.

Stories shared most often are those which we were not laughing at the time they were happening. For some reason most of these types of stories in my life are about my daughter. Like when she used a permanent marker on my mom's piano and within the next couple hours took the finger nail polish to my sister's desk or when she enjoyed painting the bathroom with toothpaste—I could smell toothpaste for days. These stories are fun and NOW they are enjoyable to share, I do have to be careful to share positive stories also, especially within earshot of my sweet children.

I try to make opportunities for my children in helping their self-esteem grow. One thing they seem to enjoy and I have been having them do since they were very young is sing together. This is something that brings much praise, not only from me but from those they sing to. It can be something as simple as singing Happy Birthday on the phone to someone. Some moments I have treasured are seeing my three older children stand in front of a congregation and sing together. I love how they do it together!

Imagine being an anthropologist and coming across the ruins of an ancient city or a paleontologist and finding bones of an undiscovered dinosaur. What a feeling of excitement and fulfillment especially after searching for so long and putting so much into your study and all of a sudden coming across something so new to your knowledge. Our children do this every day. They are constantly discovering new things. When a child comes to you and holds an object, like a rock, right up to your eye for observation, take the time to study it and realize what this means to him. In a couple minutes that rock will be just that—a rock, but at that very moment it is an ancient city or the undiscovered dinosaur bone—treasure it as your child does.

Sometimes the things our children are discovering are not always the easiest to allow them to discover. Such as a son or daughter bringing home a snake to show you, I haven't had that one yet, that is one of my fears. I do remember one of my sons trying to touch a spider with his little finger—why not if it's not poisonous. I try to encourage my children to hold a worm, not mentioning that there is no way I would be holding it if I didn't have my garden gloves on. I also encourage them to have Dad show them how to hold and gut the fish while I comfortably watch. The other day my one year old saw a praying mantis. I watched to see what he would do. He reached and tried to pick it up and it jumped. I don't know if the praying mantis actually pinched him or just scared him as he didn't expect it to move, but he screamed and was cautious the rest of the day about going out on the patio.

There are things our children discover we need to be cautious of. Like the toilet plunger which I found my one-year-old putting his face into. I calmly took it away as I got him interested in something else. We need to be careful how we react because when we cause a lot of attention to be drawn to what we don't want them to have they will go for that object over and over again. Save the attention for things you don't mind them discovering. When they discover items that are hazardous take time to explain at their level why they shouldn't have that. Help them to understand.

There is a video I have seen about teaching children. Whenever I see a section of this video tears come to my eyes. There is a little boy skipping towards the corner of a very busy street. The mother is running after him in her bathrobe yelling at him. She finally catches him right at the corner and in a panic is yelling, "How many times have I told you not to go to the corner!" The little boy so innocently asks, "Mommy, what's a corner?" Remember to help your child understand.

Despite how hard the first few years were, I am now grateful I had my first three children so close. I love to see them enjoy each other. They will spend hours entertaining each other. Of course we have off days and moments of contention, but for the most part they are good friends. Along with my three grade-schoolers I have a one-year-old and in a few months will add a newborn. It has been amazing to me to see how much I have enjoyed this last baby and I am even enjoying this last pregnancy, of course I am over the nauseous stage and not into the huge and uncomfortable one yet. There is a joy in watching my older three love to make our one-year-old laugh. Watching them entertain one another is better than a good movie.

Just this morning I had a moment to treasure. My one-year-old has had croup for the last couple days. As I sat here writing in the wee hours of the morning, I heard him coughing again. I went up and made a steam room in the bathroom and was able to rock him for a while to help his breathing. He is now sleeping again. As much as I don't want him to be sick I can still treasure that he allowed me to rock and hold him. Treasure moments of peace also. I live for nap times where I can take a short nap myself and then spend time trying to strengthen myself through scripture reading and other good books. Take time to make time for you. This is something I am still working on. As is said, fill your own bucket. It's hard to give from a bucket that is empty. For your sake and your family's sake be sure to do some things that uplift you. It's easier to treasure each moment when you feel well and good about how life is going. Take a self-improvement course, find a hobby, relish in a good book, soak in a bubble bath. Some like to go shopping or get their nails done. I am too cheap to enjoy spending money on myself. Sometimes it pays to spend the money if it is something to help you be a better you. I am working on this one.

Treasure the opportunity you have been given to be a mother. One of the greatest blessings in my life is the decision my husband and I made for me to quit work and be at home with my children full time. This was not an easy decision. I enjoyed working and could have pursued a career in what I was doing. Financially it would have been easier for me to work. We sacrificed where we could and feeling our desires were good were blessed to have them met. This was not easy on my husband either. I am so grateful for his support. We have struggled, but through many blessed experiences have had our needs met. I feel my greatest asset is our family. Because we have sacrificed some monetary goods I have been blessed to witness each day the progress and growth of our children. This is something to be treasured. I love moments when my children come to me to share something from their day. Sometimes these shared experiences are sad and tears are shared and other times there is laughter or joy from what they share. My hope is they will always feel they can come to me with their thoughts and feelings and feel not feel threatened by my response. I want to be involved in their lives, yet allow them to learn from their own decisions and consequences. Being at home for them all the time gives me more opportunities to do this.

I also treasure the opportunity this gives me to be involved in their schools. I love getting to know the students in their classes. I have been able to share babysitting with friends. This allows us each to have the time and ability to spend time in their school classes. Being involved in the PTA is also a good thing and can help improve the schools our children attend. It is also a good way to get to know other mothers to join your support group. Some days I wonder if I should be so involved—remember if it is taking too much from your family, it is okay to say no. Family is first!

As a mother I also encourage my kids to share what they tell or show me with their dad. Sometimes I hint to my husband to ask a certain child about such and such a thing. That way he is also involved in their lives. My husband is very good at spending time with us as a family when he is home. I love to watch him play football or baseball in our backyard, which attracts a neighborhood of kids. This is yet another moment to treasure. I can maybe even like Nintendo when I see him playing it with our boys—I wouldn't go as far as saying I treasure it though.

Allow your husband to watch the kids. Give him moments to treasure. He may complain about how the baby cried the whole time you were gone, but how is he going to have "moments" if you don't allow him to try his own hand at parenting.

Treasure your friends and the moments you have with them. I feel pain and anguish inside as I see a friend suffer. It is these moments that actually bring us closer as we share our weakest hours. Don't just take time to help clean and do laundry, but sit and listen, hug and share.

My last two pregnancies have been shared with a dear friend who has been pregnant with me. It is great to have someone to complain to who understands and feels exactly what you are going through. We laugh and cry together. She has an awful time with her pregnancies—more so than myself. What is amazing to me is that as I laid on her bed with her being so sick, not being able to eat without it coming back up she shared what a wonderful gift it is to carry such a child. Here we were literally in the depths of misery and she was treasuring the moment. Carrying a child is a moment to be treasured. Not all have that opportunity given to them. I need to be thankful for each movement I feel from inside as this baby grows. Once this baby is born I may never feel that again.

The most precious time to me is just before I go to bed. I usually go into each of my children's rooms to see them sleeping. It is at these times I have been overcome with the love of a mother. No matter what transpired throughout a day the sight of a sleeping child erases all frustration and replaces love. I remember one night going in to look at my boys. As I watched them sleep my heart was once again overcome with love. As I watched them I realized I too had a mother who loved me. I could picture her doing the same. This realization brought tears to my eyes and a feeling that I too was loved as I love my children. I am thankful God has given me this great opportunity!

All in all as mothers we have a lot to cherish. Even our trials can be cherished. I have come closer to my husband through struggling with him. My closest friends are those who have seen me at my darkest moments. Even struggles my children go through have enhanced our relationship as I have shown sympathy for what they are going through.

Our greatest trials usually bring us closer to God and our friends. This is a good thing—treasure it!

Chapter 5

"WHOA!" HOW DO I PUT A REIN ON THESE EMOTIONS?

My sister called me the other day regarding frustrations in being a mother of a one-month-old baby. She had to have her gallbladder removed three weeks after her baby was born. She had just gotten her baby to sleep for longer periods of time and then the surgery threw off the schedule. As I talked to her about her dilemma she mentioned how she is so close to tears all the time. Boy did that bring back memories. At this point you need to realize all your body has been through. For the first few weeks after childbirth you are still recovering. There is pain involved with this; cramping, back ache, nursing. While trying to recover there is the fact of sheer exhaustion. You are most likely sleeping less now than you were when you were burdened with the aches and pains of being pregnant. Let it out! You have a reason to be emotional. This is also a good time to look to a support group. Suck in a bit of that pride and allow others to help. Whether it be a mom, your husband or a friend, allow them to watch the baby while you rest for a spell.

I haven't had to have a gallbladder removed after a pregnancy, but I have had mastitis once or twice after each birth. This takes over my whole body and forces me to depend on others. I passed out one of the times I went through this. Thank goodness my husband was there to catch me. One thing I gain during this physical trial is that it forces me to rest—which is needed to recover. It has also brought feelings of love from others. This kind of sounds like I want bad things to happen so others will show pity and love. That's not what I mean. The last time I had mastitis I was in a state of exhaustion. My body was still recovering from the pregnancy. I had four children and a home I was trying to take care of. I was frustrated at what I couldn't accomplish. This was when friends stepped in and helped. I still wanted to be able to do it all myself, but this was a moment where I felt love from my friends and was grateful for them in my life.

Overwhelmed with not being able to accomplish all I wanted to or anything for that matter with my little kids around, I noticed the words to a song I had playing. It brought tears to my eyes, that's right—there go the emotions. This song is by Lynne Perry Christofferson, a Christian song writer.

Keeping Sheep

I have a little flock of sheep

and they are mine to tend and keep.

And I must guard them every day

for little lambs, when left alone, will lose their way.

So many voices say to me,

A sheep fold is no place to be.

Your time in there is dull and slow,

and lambs leave very little room for you to grow.

Chorus

Oh (So), if I ever start to stray,

Deceived by thoughts of greener pastures,

Remind me, Lord, that keeping sheep

will lead to happier ever-afters.

Will lead to happier ever-afters.

Oh, surely there will come a day

When all the lambs have left my side,

And I am free to roam about,

And go exploring other meadows,

Green and wide.

Yet something whispers in my heart

That when my sheep have left this pen

I'll long to stroke their little heads,

To draw them close to me

And have them young again.

Repeat Chorus

So while they still are in my care

I pray that I will clearly see

these little lambs within my fold

are tender gifts the Master Shepherd

has given me.

(Lynn Perry Christofferson, "Keeping Sheep", CD Keeping Sheep, Prime Recordings Inc. 2001 1-800-377-6788)

We get so overwhelmed with all we have to do as mothers of young children, but deep down we also know they won't always be this way. Part of us wants them to grow and the other part wants them to stay small. No wonder our emotions get the better of us.

I tend to suppress my emotions. My husband tries to get me to show excitement. He enjoys life and it shows. When you give him a gift he likes you know it. When he gives me a gift I love, I don't outwardly express my excitement as he would and he apologizes for not getting what I wanted. The funny thing is my mom is more like my husband in this way. She gets excited over the changing of the seasons and everyone knows it. She'll dance with my kids in the fall leaves. She loves to share it with all. I love the changing of the seasons, but I enjoy it inside with a feeling of peace at realizing what is going on around me. I don't think either reaction is right or wrong, just the way we are.

One thing I do, but don't feel is quite right, is hold in my frustrations and worries. Growing up I rarely expressed these to others. The strange thing is that others seem to unload theirs on me. It has been through my husband and good friends that I am slowly learning to release these and open up to others. I remember sobbing into my pillow many nights. That was my release. A few months after we were married I had one of these release moments. The only problem was that my pillow was right next to my husband's. It was the first time he'd seen me break down and really cry. He was sure something was drastically wrong. I'm sure he was ready to take me to a hospital or admit me into a mental institution. Since then, these moments of crying and opening up to him have been some of our most intimate and have brought us closer.

Crying together as friends brings us closer. One night I became aware that a friend's husband was in the hospital again. She has had her share of life struggles and I knew her last straw was about ready to break. I found some inspirational books to take to her and went to her house. It was there I stayed until late in the evening as we cried together. I couldn't do anything to take away her problems, but I could listen and cry with her. This was a bonding time for both of us. These moments shared are not soon forgotten. Bonds of friendship are strengthened.

Laughter is also an emotion when shared bonds us together. Even at moments when tears are being shared a few laughs pop in from viewing the events. Picture two mothers sitting on a couch. Both nursing their fourth babies while discussing frustrations. Obviously exhausted from the woes of motherhood and just plain life situations when in mid-sentence the one stops talking. Lo and behold she had fallen asleep—mid-sentence. What a moment to share!

I have no idea as to what causes this flow of emotions to come on. Take this for instance. I was left without a car, which was fine because I had adjusted my schedule. When I got back from walking, my third grader phoned to tell me her ear was really hurting. She had complained about it in the morning, but I thought I'd give it some time. Not having a car, I walked over to the school to give her some ear drops. I phoned the doctor to see when I could get her in, but I didn't have a car to get her there and the only doctor available was one I didn't want to see. So, do I put off having her see a doctor until tomorrow or do I get on the phone with the "support system" of friends I have and borrow a car? This mixture of decisions to make put me in a frenzy and I began to cry. So, I did the best thing I could—I took a nap. When I woke up I felt much better although no decision was made.

Another day I was waiting patiently for my car to be fixed. After an hour and a half of waiting and discovering no one had even looked at my vehicle it was all I could do to ask them for my vehicle back and allow my husband to take care of it without crying. Although maybe something would have gotten done if I'd broken down and cried in front of them! It's little things like this that can ruin a day if we let it.

I don't know how to completely solve these little "mental breakdowns", but I do know that having someone to talk to about them helps. You are not the only one having them, and sometimes just knowing it's not just you going crazy helps.

Find the humor in these breakdowns. You may have to wait a day or two to do so. I remember two years ago, I was in the first trimester of my fourth child. (Note the two years ago, I can laugh now.) My energy was nonexistent, I received a call from a neighbor shortly after I had sent my kids to school. My son had stumbled while running to school. The neighbor tried to love him and give him a bandaid, but he was in hysterics. I ran over and got him calmed down. I sat on the curb with him and tried to get him to go to school. I was still in my pajamas and wasn't thrilled about the idea of going into the school. He really wanted me to walk him in. So the two of us sat on the curb and cried together. Once we both calmed down I swallowed my pride and walked him to school. It makes me smile to picture the two of us crying together on the curb.

Another day I cried because I forgot it was pajama day. The night before I had washed the pajamas to be worn and then in the rush of the morning forgot. I felt as if I had ruined the life of my kindergartener. He took it far better than I did.

When I was younger I was terrified at the thought of crying in front of others. From the time I was in grade school I remember crying my frustrations into my pillow at night. That way no one else saw or knew I was upset. Very few friends through high school and college ever saw me cry. Becoming pregnant and then attaching motherhood onto that, tears came much more frequently. I blame this overflow of emotions on being pregnant or nursing. I am not a doctor, but I know the hormones just aren't quite where they should be.

My problem is that I hold my emotions inside until finally they burst. Pregnancy and motherhood bring on a whole new list of emotions. It was a lot more to hold inside and I started breaking down more often. I have realized I need to allow these feelings to go and communicate with others about the way I feel. Whether it's frustrations, worries or plain old orneriness you need to talk about these to others. It has always helped me to write them down or address them in my prayers. But it also helps to have friends who relate to being mothers and seem to understand what you are feeling.

The other day I received a phone call from a friend. She asked what I was doing and if she could come over to talk. I wondered what had gone drastically wrong, but as she came over and began to visit I realized she just needed a companion to be with and vent a few frustrations to, just to talk with someone who understands what you feel. To have a friend to call at such times makes a big difference in my life. I have found I break down more when I don't feel well or am under more stress than usual. Whenever something is amiss in my life—like I'm worried I have offended a friend or have allowed another's actions to offend me, it eats at me and only takes something small to tip the rocker so to speak. When I take the time in a day to uplift myself with an inspirational article, read my scriptures, and say my prayers I am able to undertake a bit more. When I am focused on what I can do for others instead of what is wrong in my own life I am also uplifted and am able to handle what is handed to me.

The older I get, the more people I meet and realize there are much worse situations I could be in. I have learned to overcome a lot of my worries. We worry and worry and all it gives us is a headache. All we can do is our best for that day and tomorrow that day will be over. We may need to take a look at our lives and prioritize. Allow a few things to go. I was talking to a friend about singing in a choir. She sounded excited to be participating in it. When I didn't see her at the practice I let her know she was missed. She informed me she had committed to not take on any more "projects" in her life at the moment and had forgotten. Sometimes we need to do this. Simplify our lives. Most likely you will have to choose between good things.

Business is a big trial in the lives of mothers nowadays. We rush about from place to place and with our cell phones anyone can track us down at any given moment. Although it caused stressful moments when we only had one vehicle I have counted it a blessing in my life. It forced me to slow down, stay home and enjoy what I had. I walked a lot more to get to places and I had to plan out my days carefully if I really did need to be somewhere at a certain time.

There are emotions of being overwhelmed. As mothers we have a lot on our plate. We have a family that depends on us. One of the problems I have is a hard time saying no. If I feel someone needs my help I attempt to rearrange my schedule so I can be of help. This has caused some stressful situations and when a mother is stressed a whole family suffers. This is more to myself than anyone else—it is okay to say I can't do such and such right now just because my "plate" is full.

Usually when I feel I can't handle another thing the guilt sets in that I am not capable of handling "everything!" Guess what, there are not many who can completely handle "everything". That's why we need each other. I felt so good when I asked a favor of a friend and she explained to me all that was going on in her week. I told her not to worry about it, I could easily call someone else. She was willing but I am glad she was honest with me about how she was feeling. She didn't have any one big thing going on, just lots of little things. Those little things can add up and totally deplete the energy we have.

Thank goodness for friends and moments of emotion we can share. Don't keep these moments to yourself. Share with a friend and they will most likely understand and share with you. Other than the headaches and swollen eyes, it can actually be fun to cry together. Usually such moments of emotion bring on laughter and in the end our problems don't seem so big. Allow the reins to go loose on this one and eventually the tears won't come quite as often. It was wonderful when I realized I wasn't crying every day, I was actually enjoying life being a mother. Remember, this didn't happen overnight.

This chapter is a bit scatterbrained, but I guess that's just how a mother's emotions are—so it fits!

Chapter 6

P-A-T-I-E-N-C-E

Patience is a word I have always had a hard time spelling, it just doesn't sound like it is spelled. Isn't the English language great! Just wait until you start trying to teach your child to sound out words. Patience is a word I now practice spelling in my mind many times a day. An example of when appropriate to use: The phone rang, I picked it up in the kitchen which had a short cord. While on the phone my two-year-old daughter decided she was thirsty. Attempting to get my attention I suppose, she got the pitcher of purple punch out of the fridge, looked at me, making sure she had my attention and slowly started to pour it on my white rug. By the time I got to her the pitcher was empty. This is when you start to spell leaving a second between each letter and taking deep breaths: P-A-T-I-E-N-C-E. Usually by the time you get to the second E you can refrain from killing or maybe the child has ran off by then and saved her own life. I've tried counting to 10 also, but spelling this word helps me try to actually have some.

This may also help with a husband who can sleep through any sound a child makes. If you spell really slow maybe, just maybe, he'll wake up before you finish and get the child himself. But, most likely it will just remind you that patience is supposed to be a virtue and you will end up getting the child yourself. Most likely by morning you will still love and cherish the man who slept so well.

Not only is patience needed with most situations in life, but especially with being a mother. As I pray for my children I am most often overcome with a desire to show love to them. This is not a perfect world we live in. There are so many negative thoughts and actions going on around us. It is my desire that what my children feel from me be positive. This does not mean I don't discipline. On the contrary, discipline if done in an act of love will enhance love and respect in your relationship with children, don't forget the word LOVE in there. To show discipline with love takes a load of patience!

Have you ever felt as if your blood was boiling? There are times when I can't think straight because I get so frustrated and angry at what my kids are doing. This happens most often in the mornings when I am trying to get them to get ready for school and get jobs done before they leave. The other morning I had to literally put myself in timeout so I wouldn't do something to my children I would regret. I locked myself in my room and tried to cool down. Before they left for school I made myself tell each one I love them. I'm afraid my heart wasn't fully in it, but I couldn't bear the thought of them leaving for a whole day thinking their mother was angry with them. Although, it was a good thing they were going to school and I had a few hours to recover.

These are times when I have to make myself think, "It's not the worst thing if they go to school with a hair-do they did themselves". Or, "What they are wearing is modest—it may not match, but it covers their bodies and they like it." My mom taught me this. I had a sister and people would comment often on what she wore. She was an original—she has accomplished much in life. I now have a daughter who is a lot like her. My daughter at the age of nine has a desire to be a clothes designer. I try to encourage her. She's actually pretty good at matching, but some of the combinations she comes up with would never have come to my mind. She will go far someday too.

The first day of school is always fun to see the kids so excited to go. All are dolled up in their new school clothes their mom's have bought. This last year my third started kindergarten. I had to talk him into letting me walk him since he's quite independent. I had gotten him some new school clothes, but he insisted on wearing his worn orange "zipper pants" along with an old shirt he liked. This is also the same child who likes to wear his hair like a mad scientist—that is what he calls it too. It's not worth the fight—so what if he looks like I couldn't afford new school clothes and don't take the time to comb my kid's hair? On the walk to school I started talking to another mother, my pride set in, I mentioned to her how I had tried to get him to wear his new school clothes and she proceeded to tell me how she was still new at this and made her kids dress up. I guess part of patience is setting aside the thought of what others might think. Why did I need to explain to another mother why my kid looked the way he did? I knew why he looked that way. It makes me smile to see such a personality come out.

I remember one morning the events were such I had to hop out of the picture, look at the situation and laugh. I thought I had recorded it in my journal, but I haven't been able to find the account. It included all three of my children crying at once. Something like my daughter had been scared by a bug and about the same time my son who was newly potty trained had fallen back into the toilet and was stuck—I can't remember why the baby was crying. I just remember sitting in the hall with my three crying children and chuckling at the situation I was in. These weren't events I was mad about, they just happened. I could have sat in the hall and cried with them—I've done that before, but for some reason I was able to patiently sit down and realize the humor in the situation.

Have you ever noticed it is at bedtime when your children want to share anything and everything with you? It's at this time I am so ready to have them in bed and sit and relax in peace and silence. By this time my patience is worn out, my voice seems to get louder especially when they get back out of bed to ask for one more thing. As I tucked my daughter in last night she told me she didn't fit into this family. I asked her why. She said it was because every time she was scared at night and tried to come down and talk to us Dad would yell at her. I explained to her how early her dad rises in the morning (3:30 AM) and by night time we are tired and just need to relax and rest. We know she is safe and all is well she just needs to go to sleep.

I have also noticed when I do keep my patience and allow myself to sit and listen to my children at night I can learn a lot from them. I have not been good at this lately. I have a son who is not very free with his words. You ask him a question and it is most often answered with a blank stare. Neighbors tell me he will come over to their house, knock on the door and then just stand there without saying a word. Assuming that he is there to play with one of their children they usually let him in. He is getting better at this, but at times we feel it would be easier to pull teeth than get an answer out of him. It is at night when I am tucking him in that he decides to open up. He tells me everything from what happened at school that day to what he wants for breakfast the next morning.

If I could just make the most of this time I could get a lot out of it. When I take time to actually ask questions of how the day went or what they did at a certain friend's house I can learn a lot about my children. It is my goal to allow this to happen more often in the evenings and hopefully it will be a time my children feel they can open up to their dad and I. All it takes is a little more patience before the day ends. My desire is this will carry on to when they are in their teen years.

Talk about teen years. I am not there yet, but as I hear parents talk of what it's like to have a teenager I feel like they are talking about my nine-year-old daughter and she has been this way since she was two! I love my daughter so very much and am so thankful to have her, but she seems to know how to make my patience fly out the door. My hope is she will get her attitude resolved now and her teen years will be enjoyable, most just laugh when I say this. In a few years I guess I'll know why they are laughing.

You can't have a book on being a mother without mentioning toilet training. This is something where patience is definitely needed. In fact I have found, as I have potty trained three now, that if you're patient enough and let them do it on their own time it is much more successful. After they are finally trained is when true patience is needed since they always have to make a potty stop just after you have left the house or when you have just arrived at a park without an open bathroom. Sometimes I wonder why I took them out of diapers—wouldn't it be easier to just teach them how to change their own. Although it is nice when you don't have to pay for diapers each month.

Food is also something we need patience with. With my first born I was experimenting with different kinds of foods when she was three months old. With my fourth I was hesitant to start at six months. It just means more messes to clean up. That's one thing about food and a family. It seems like I am buying it, preparing it, or cleaning it up at all times of the day. I have been reminded of how children learn to eat since my 18 month old insists on feeding himself now. It is so cute to watch him dig into his meal attempting to use the spoon but mostly using his hands. My floor has to be mopped after every meal. When I am thinking of what to fix for a meal I quite often consider what mess it will cause. Spaghetti—prepare to do an overhaul afterwards. Corn Dogs, on the other hand, tend to be much cleaner as long as you don't offer ketchup with it.

As my kids get older they seem to be pickier on what they will or will not eat. Maybe I caused this since I am a slightly picky eater. My husband hates to order food for me. He says he always gets it wrong. Nevertheless it is still frustrating to fix a meal for a family, there is always at least one complaint. Find comfort in thinking someday they will be in charge of cooking a meal themselves. It helped our family to have everyone help plan the meals. Each person has a night of the week and they get to choose what to have that night. That way everyone is happy with dinner at least once during the week.

Every life situation seems to need patience. It is so easy to always say, "It will be so much better when my baby sleeps through the night." Or, "I will be happier when we can afford to have a budget." There are always things to hope and wish for. It's good to have hope, but we can be happy with what we have now. I guess it is easier to have patience when we attempt to treasure the moments we are living. Patience in our trials is a hard one. We want all the answers now. Isn't it interesting how as young couples we look at our parents and want all they have now. We need to realize they didn't have all they have now, when they were newly married with young children. We had a neighborhood progressive dinner the other night. At the last host's house there was Christmas décor everywhere. We tease that there is a glow that comes from this home because of all the lights. She even has a life size snowman that sings when you walk up to the door. It was fun to see all she had. As we finished our desert the host explained to us how she didn't always have all that we could see. It had been from years and years of collecting. Her children are grown now. She told of a Christmas season twenty-six years earlier that was spent in the hospital with a sick child. They came home from the hospital shortly before Christmas. There were only Charlie Brown trees left in the lot.   Gifts found under their tree that year came from neighbors and friends. She says this was her most memorable Christmas. How blessed they must have felt to just be together for the holiday, to still have their son with them.

Somehow we seem to get through our trials—it just takes a little patience, open eyes and a few good friends to share them with.

Chapter 7

CHERISH YOUR SPOUSE

I know none of you can have a husband as wonderful as mine cause I have him. My husband is very supportive in all that I do. We are very close. It is true, we need a support system of other mothers, but never let that overtake the friendship and openness you have with your spouse. He is the father of your children and I believe should be your best friend. You have a long road to haul together. Obviously there will be bumps in the road and rocks to climb over, but never close the communication gap between the two of you.

In reading an article by a religious leader a couple of years ago I came across the phrase, "Cherish your spouse". It was such a simple phrase, but it hit me hard. At the time I was nitpicking at all the little things he didn't do or what he did do but not the way I wanted it done. I hadn't actually voiced my complaints, but was just plain ornery with him and he didn't know why. At that time I began to add in my prayers for help in knowing how to "Cherish" my spouse. As I focused on that phrase I was able to notice all the good he did.

What does this have to do with being a mother? Everything! You wouldn't be a mother if he wasn't a father. God kind of planned it this way. It's actually a pretty good plan. As mother and father we have different but equal roles in a family. Learn and do things together. Appreciate the differences.

I recently spent a week with my sister and her husband. She was in the nitpicking phase. I heard myself give her the advice to allow him to do it in his own way. Give him an evening with the child without you. My husband tells me many times that the second I go out the door the child or children act differently. That may be but I think the second that he walks in the door the kids seem to have more respect for their mother. We have to learn to deal with this whatever the case. I am told that I walk out the door and the baby starts crying, I walk back in and not a cry is heard. I tease my husband that the baby just doesn't like what he's watching on T.V. I could tell him all that I do to try to help him be more successful when I am out, but whatever he does he's not going to be Mom. He's Dad—he's got to find his own way to be successful at this parenthood thing.

My daughter got a book at the school library a couple weeks ago. It was one of those books your kids ask you to read ten times a day. I was ready to send it back to school, but it was a cute book. I think it was called Octopus Hugs. Dad is home babysitting for the night and the little sister is sad about Mom being gone. So Dad begins by giving octopus hugs. One arm around here, the other arm around there and so forth. He then proceeds to play numerous games with the kids like rocking in a rocking chair that keeps rocking them out or being a ride they pretend to put a quarter into to make it go. The night goes on with such games. What would the night have been like if Mom had stayed home? Allow Dad to enjoy his kids in his own great way!

I love the way my husband plays with our kids. We finally got grass in our backyard this last summer. Most evenings after he came home from work you could find him out back immersed in a game of baseball, football or basketball with our boys and any other neighbor kids in the area who happened by. When occasionally he lies on the grass to rest you can bet someone is going to tackle him.

My husband is also a very good teacher. I love how he teaches our children to work. He has been the one to have them do the dishes and not only do them, but work together to get them done. We have been finishing our basement. There is a lot of pounding that goes on down there. He has allowed our kids to help. I realized one day all the pounding was our kids and one of their friends attempting to pound in a nail. This nail could have been within seconds by my husband, but he was allowing them to use their own hammers and help in the work.

The other day I was in a state of desperation. My two oldest children had been fighting quite a bit for the last couple of days. I felt they needed a job where they had to actually work together. I turned to my husband and explained my feelings. He thought for a moment and then said, "I've got it!" He sent them down into the window wells to clean them out. They had to work together to clean out what garbage was in them and then to help each other clean the spots on the windows including the hard water stains. The best part of it was that he supervised the work being done. Sometimes just getting them to get the job done is not worth the effort—I am thankful for his efforts in this.

Not every man is going to be like my husband, but every man is still a child of God and has qualities that are good. Remember, you fell in love with him for some reason. I know of husbands who are expert cleaners—be thankful for this. It's easy to see what drives you crazy about your spouse, be a bigger person and discover what you love about him.

I am not a therapist or psychologist, but I would guess communication is one of the biggest reasons spouses don't get along. I have enjoyed a class on relationships lately. It has brought to my attention that I am a "hinter". As my husband watches television, which is his way to relax and release the tension and stress in his life, I may be doing dishes or laundry and feel I would like his help. Instead of voicing my desire I bang the dishes as loud as I can or I make it a point to walk right by him with a HEAVY load of laundry adding a grunt or two in there. The first problem with this is that it is pointless. If a good show is on there is no way he will notice or hear my plights of plea. All it does is frustrate me more. The second is that I become very ornery and he has no idea why. We then have a family meeting where I address that I would like everyone's help in cleaning up each meal. Of course I am talking to the kids in hopes that he will take a hint.

In this relationship class we talked about taking words from our mouth literally. So when my husband sees how ornery I am and asks, "Are you okay?" or "What is wrong?" and I say, "I am fine." He can take me literally and it is my fault for not voicing my concerns. In other words, quit playing the guessing game. It saves a lot of time and effort to get worries and concerns out there and discuss them. Sure my husband will probably be happy to help with cleaning up, but he will also voice to me that he would like to watch a show or game without being disturbed or being made to feel guilty for laying down to watch it.

What is it we tell our kids?—cooperate, work it out together. It's a give and take situation. We both need each other and we both need time for our own desires to be met. Allow for him to create and pursue his own hobbies and talents as he will hopefully allow the same for you. Also find hobbies you can do together.

My husband does woodworking on the side. I am not a woodworker, but I do spend quite a bit of time with him when he's working to help hold a board or to be a "listening board". I guess this is how I support this hobby. I do benefit from the beautiful things he makes for our home.

We also enjoy doing yard work together. We have worked hard to put a yard in and every year we plan out and put in a garden which we enjoy taking care of. It's fun to see the results of our work at the end of each summer. My husband gets so excited when the first tomato comes on. I always try to allow him to be the first to discover it.

Occasionally we golf together. I am not a great golfer, but Rex enjoys it and my family encourages it. I was raised by a mother who loves golfing. I remember waking up summer mornings to a note from my mom that she was out golfing and would be home shortly. When we go on vacations with my family we golf—thus I have learned how to golf, I just haven't perfected the sport yet. I do enjoy doing it with my husband. It gives us time to be together without kids and enjoying one another.

One of my hobbies is music. My husband has been a good sport especially when I have offered our family to perform musical numbers. He has sung with our children quite a few times. He actually enjoys singing and I think he is quite good at it, he just lacks the confidence of knowing he is good. I believe that would be called being humble—another attribute he has.

Whatever your situation, likes or dislikes, discover what you can do to support your spouse in the things he enjoys and find some you can do together. Remember the "take time to make time" for yourself, well also "take time to make time" for your spouse and help enhance your relationship. Not only will you be helping your life to be more bearable, but it will also bless the lives of your children.

From friends I have learned of something called "LOVE WEEK". This is where you spend a week of doing little extras for your spouse. You can make this a big production or just do minor things throughout the week to show a little extra LOVE. My husband's birthday is a week before Valentine's Day so last year I tried that week. It turned out to be a lot of fun. My kids even got involved in it and by the end of the week my husband was returning the actions. Each morning I had a new message written with lipstick on the mirror. In his lunch I would pack a special note and treat. A friend gave me the idea to put sexy underwear in with his lunch one day. Dinner was prepared and waiting for him when he got home, I tried to fix some of his favorite meals. Then I did something special for him each day like a heart attack in our bedroom. The kids had a riot helping me with this one as they helped cut out paper hearts and tape them all over our room. I sent him flowers at work one day. I ironed his shirts, this is something he usually does himself. Use your imagination and do the unexpected. It's well worth your time and effort since LOVE is usually returned!

It's so easy as a mother of young children to feel overwhelmed. We tend to take our frustrations out on those closest to us—our children and husband. Don't push away your greatest strength. Stay close to him and help him realize what you might be feeling. This is hard since as women we don't even know ourselves what we are feeling sometimes. Help him to understand this and hopefully he will be more understanding with you.

I am so thankful for a loving and supportive husband. He is my best friend. I love how he supports and understands the need I have for a support group of friends. He has been known to call one of my friends to ask if she could get me out of the house. He seems to recognize when I am beginning to go slightly crazy and need to step out of the routine of motherhood. He even offers to watch my friend's kids when necessary to help me be able to get out with a friend.

I am thankful for the great opportunity of cherishing my spouse. It blesses my life to realize the prize I won when I married him. Sure we have our differences and we don't agree on everything, but when we are cherishing one another it is easier to overcome these. Begin today by finding something to cherish about your spouse.

Chapter 8

"IT'S JUST A PHASE"

In complaining to a friend about certain situations my kids are in, whether it's my son eating dirt or a child having accidents, she has often commented to me, "It's just a phase, they'll get over it."

This is true—it goes back to that patience thing and realizing by the time they are twenty they probably won't be doing whatever is driving me crazy at the moment. Of course they will most likely be doing something else which I don't agree with. I know my parents still don't agree with all I do.

I need to sit back and take a look at what I get so frustrated with and if it is really worth the worry. What's that quote about worrying? Something about worry being the interest you pay. It is so true, no matter how much I worry they will still do whatever I worry about and eventually time will pass and they will be on to something new.

Choose your fights carefully. A phase of hitting probably needs to be addressed since it involves those he/she hits. A phase of picking a nose will most likely pass. I love my friend's quote, "Don't pick your nose in public." Go right ahead and pick your nose, just don't do it where others can see.

It makes me smile to think of the phases my kids have gone through. I still have marks of a phase of coloring on the wall. I remember being so frustrated with it and no matter what I did for discipline whether it be time-out or having her clean it herself I continued to find more artwork. She still enjoys being an artist, but now it is usually done on the proper paper. Another phase that I think many kids go through at one time or another is not eating. I love my pediatrician. He is the one who has stressed to me to have a set place and time for meals and eating and then allow the child to eat or not eat as they will. If you can really follow this it relieves a lot of stress. First of all it keeps the mess of food to one place. It also helps to not have to have food prepared twenty-four seven. Most likely the child will eat when they get hungry. Forcing them to eat won't serve you or them.

There are lots of other phases. We don't all experience all of them, but we do all experience some. Like bed wetting, eating snow, opening doors he shouldn't go out, running into the street, eating dirt, a colicky baby (this has got to be a hard one!), illnesses like ear aches, sleeplessness, nightmares, the list goes on and on.

One phase I think everyone goes through with every child is tantrums. If you're lucky this is a short phase, but some last longer. I think this is where the name of "terrible twos" comes from. From my experience the "terrible twos" start at about 18 months. A child is beginning to discover and realize he can go further and do more all on his own. It's actually quite amusing the things they discover at this time. I am amazed to watch my toddler as he pushes a chair to what he wants. He has recently discovered the bar stool can get him higher, so he will push the barstool to what he wants and then push a chair to the barstool. Isn't this a sign of a smart kid? Too bad it doesn't always amuse me especially when he gives himself a bath in the kitchen sink or climbs to where the knives are. It seems like lately I am constantly saying no to him or taking away something else.

I have found the best way to handle these tantrums is to ignore them. Definitely don't give in to a tantrum, that is telling your child he can get what he wants by screaming. When my first three were all so young I found that vacuuming helped me ignore these tantrums. This accomplished two things, first it kept my house clean, second I couldn't hear their screaming.

There are phases to enjoy also, like a child reading books. I love to see a little one who can't read sit with a book in front of them and turn the pages. The snuggling stage is a fun one too, you can never get too many loves from a child. I love the phase right before a baby is mobile. It's such a fun age, they can't get into much trouble and they are usually full of smiles and laughs. These stages don't seem to last long enough. Schedules also seem to go into phases. That's one thing with a child—a schedule is great and every child and mother needs one, but they also get interrupted or change frequently. Adjust! Like a schedule with nap times. We have to work into our day nap times. First they nap in and out all day then usually you can get on a routine of two naps a day, then down to one and eventually none. It's the "none" phase that kills me. I demanded a quiet time especially when I had younger ones that still required naps.

Potty training. Thank goodness this one is just a phase. Although this phase can last much too long! I've heard it said that you urge and urge your child to tell you when they have to go to the bathroom, when they finally learn how to go on their own you spend the next couple years letting them know they don't need to inform you—just go! Like I read in a book recently, "Yes, your perspective changes as you gain more experience as a parent. For example, for the first few years of your parenting career, you spend untold hours coaxing your children to talk and walk. Then you spend the rest of your life trying to get them to sit down and hush up." (Grin and Share It, pg. ?)

All in all childhood is "just a phase". Any mother whose children are all grown will tell you to enjoy them for they won't stay young for long. This is our challenge—enjoy each phase despite the frustrations and great demands that come with these young children.

Chapter 9

CALM "DURING" THE STORM

You've heard of the calm before the storm. In the life of a mother this is the silence you notice just before you discover why there was silence. Upon discovering this scene, spell our word, P A T I E N C E. Okay, now is the time to allow the calm "during " the storm.

The summer before I got married I had the opportunity to work at an outdoor learning center. That year was a very wet one. It stormed most of the days throughout the beginning of the summer. We worked out in the weather every day and sometimes slept outside in it. As long as we had on the right gear it could be enjoyed. I now love taking walks in the rain. I learned to enjoy the storms. I even enjoy watching lightning from a safe spot. I have a fond memory of staying at my Grandma's house during a lightning storm. She opened her curtains and we watched the storm together. I do admit some storms are better enjoyed from a warm safe spot, like a winter blizzard.

Storms of motherhood rarely have a warm safe spot they can be watched from and walking leisurely through them with enjoyment is out of the question. We can, however, try to remain calm and turn these storms into teaching or bonding moments instead of natural disasters. We may need to remove ourselves from the situation if possible, take a deep breath and then act.

When my third was born my first was still two. We were living in an old home with some steep steps going up to the bedrooms. My baby was about two weeks old and asleep in his bassinet. When I went in to check on him he was gone. I began looking frantically for him and finally found him upstairs with my two-year-old daughter. She had wanted him to sleep in her bed, so she carried him up the steep steps of the old house we lived in. By the time I found her I was so upset, somehow I was able to remain calm. I sat down with her at that moment, put her hands up to mine and explained how big my hands were compared to hers. I tried to teach her why I didn't want her carrying the baby. Now, if I had screamed at her it would not have become a teaching moment. Have you ever thought that maybe, as mothers, we sometimes cause storms? There have been many situations where I have blown up at my kids with a raised voice. Usually at these moments I am angry and not thinking clearly. I find myself saying things that make absolutely no sense. At these moments nothing is being taught, my kids just want to get away from me. They want to go to a "warm safe spot". Shouldn't that spot be in our homes? This calm has a lot to do with exercising the P word, patience.

There are many instances I can recall where I did not keep my cool. Such as when I had just swept the kitchen floor for the fourth time that morning and the next thing I knew my toddler opened the pantry door and poured dry oatmeal all over the floor. I yelled at him that I was so tired of finding a new mess every time I turned around. Obviously he didn't understand what I was yelling about. He was definitely not receiving any comfort from me at that point!

Why is it that once a storm hits, other storms hit on top of it. Like this day, my one-year-old was quiet as I was setting the table for dinner. Usually he is crying at my feet until I feed him dinner. I heard something drop and then I heard him scream. He had gotten a candle I'd left burning (not smart on my part). From what I could tell he had tried to swallow the hot wax. I quickly grabbed him and rushed him to the sink to apply cold water to his face and get a cold drink in him while swiping wax out of his mouth. I was amazed to not find any burns. While he was still crying from this, my daughter, being a big help, got the gallon of punch out for dinner. She slipped and it went spilling to the floor. I couldn't yell at her even though I was ready to yell at somebody, she was just trying to help. To top it off, my husband was out of town until the next day. We managed to get through dinner, but by bedtime I was ready for a break and proceeded to scream while trying to get the kids in bed.

I'm sure as mothers every single one of us have numerous accounts we can share of days or moments similar to this.

I have been blessed, knock on wood, that we have never had to rush a child to the emergency room. But, we have had our share of blood along with a few broken bones. Thank goodness for after hours at the clinic. It's at these moments a mom must stay calm. Causing a storm at a time like this will only make matters worse. If panic sets in, irrational actions can cause more damage. At this point I am usually praying non-stop in my head. If a mother can stay calm it will help everyone else to be calm too. Can you imagine what my son, who screams like he is dying when in pain or within sight of his own blood, would do if I gasped at an injury of his? He'd probably pass out!

It is ironic how a mother is the one to set the mood in a household. Lately our home has had some hefty storms come through. I have had to stand back and think, "What am I doing to cause them?" or "What can I do to help smooth things over?" I may need to put myself in time out for a few minutes to contemplate how I am acting. Sometimes a good walk helps clear my mind and I can be a better person to be around.

Just putting on peaceful music helps bring a different feeling to our home or an act of service done by myself or my children is another idea. Make cookies and allow your children to deliver them to whoever they think would appreciate them. With a little effort we can keep some of the storms away.

As mothers we need to make our homes be the "warm safe spot" from the storms of life. We are the ones to intervene and keep peace in our homes. One of the keys is to take care of yourself, spiritually, physically, mentally and socially, so you can be prepared for whatever challenge or "STORM" may come your way. Allowing myself to depend upon my friends and family, and knowing I can ask for help if in need, helps keep me better prepared. Realizing you are not alone can make a big difference!

Chapter 10

ENDURE!

Here I sit in the last few weeks of my fifth pregnancy. All I can think of to get me by is ENDURE! Amidst pains of pregnancy and things I would like to get done I still have four other children and a husband who have to get by. They are all being required to do a little more to help around the house. We will be able to endure better if we are in it together.

After the baby is born it will be the sleepless nights that must be endured. If we look at motherhood as a whole to endure, it will seem impossible. Look at each situation or each "phase" you are in and realize, "I can endure that much." The "one step at a time" concept helps especially in the role of being a mother. Some days that "step" may only be a few minutes long.

As Winston Churchill said, "Never, never, never give up." My husband recited to me the story of when this quote was made. Prime Minister Churchill was addressing a boy's school. He was expected to give a big eloquent speech. He stood up and said, "Never, never, never give up." He then sat down. I can imagine there was silence afterwards.

Think about those words. Think of all other mothers across the world. We each have different circumstances, different lifestyles. Some struggle more than others, some are given more diverse trials. No matter who or where we are we each have children we love and want the best for. We can never give up for their sake.

When I was in college my Grandma gave me a journal and on it was written a poem:

Don't Quit

When things go wrong as they sometimes will,

When the road you're trudging seems all uphill,

When funds are low, and the debts are high,

And you want to smile, but you have to sigh,

When care is pressing you down a bit—

Rest if you must, but don't you quit.

Success is failure turned inside out,

The silver tint of the clouds of doubt,

And you never can tell how close you are,

It may be near when it seems afar.

So, stick to the fight when you're hardest hit—

It's when things go wrong that you mustn't quit.

Author Unknown

I have read this poem often, especially when the road I seem to be trudging is so steep. I love to hike, I enjoy the fresh air and being surrounded by God's creations. Sometimes the trails we hike become steep. Just take a little bit at a time and then rest for a moment to catch your breath. It's at these moments of catching my breath I notice my surroundings the most. Eventually we reach our destination whether it is a long hike or a short one. Life's experiences are kind of like this. Some are long, some are short, but all can be endured. It's at the end of a hike when feelings of accomplishment set in.

I now have a little baby girl! That last week of my pregnancy was so long! I was experiencing contractions all week. We even went to the hospital in the middle of one night and were sent back home. In all my five pregnancies that is a first. It was so depressing to be leaving the hospital and still be pregnant! That week I had numerous friends call me to offer to take kids or to see how I was doing. I was given all kinds of advice on how to make myself go into labor, none of which worked! I told my husband we would have to send each child to a different home to take up all the offers we were given. Despite my complaints I made it! We have our fifth child. She is a healthy beautiful little girl, another miracle in our lives. Every single one of us is enjoying her, including our one year old.

It's always easier to look back after the trial and realize everything is okay. It's when we are in the midst of adversity that we need to remember, "This too shall pass." Each stage of motherhood will pass too quickly just like each phase our kids go through will also pass us by.

Remember, YOU ARE NOT ALONE! Make the effort to reach out, find a friend and work together to make the most of what you have been given.

It is my heart's desire that every mother have a friend to confide in, someone to help them along. I now have a wonderful support group in my life, but that doesn't mean I am home free. Life goes on as it always will. Changes happen. New challenges will come. I hope my circle of friends will grow.

Life is busy with five kids. Trying to get them and myself all ready for a day is possible, but I haven't figured out how to do this and then get something else accomplished. To tell you the truth I need to read this book and be reminded of what is most important. I need to let the laundry or the dishes go and call a friend for no other reason than to just talk and catch up on life and to be reminded of what a wonderful life I have with these five precious children, a wonderful spouse and friends to share it all with.

Made in the USA
Middletown, DE
06 November 2021